Original title:
The Charm of a Brooch

Copyright © 2025 Creative Arts Management OÜ
All rights reserved.

Author: Arabella Whitmore
ISBN HARDBACK: 978-1-80586-008-2
ISBN PAPERBACK: 978-1-80586-480-6

An Enchantment in Every Curve

Upon a shirt, a sparkle shines,
A little pin, with hidden lines.
It tells a tale of quirks and glee,
    A fashionista's jubilee!

Oh, what a scene, a squiggly twist,
It whispers secrets, can't be missed.
With every glance, a giggle's caught,
What wisdom in this gem has sought!

Sentinels of Style

Tiny soldiers on a vest,
In crazy shapes, they do their best.
A flamingo, a cat, perhaps a shoe,
Each boasts a story, uniquely true.

They guard the fabric, brave and bold,
Whispering tales, yet to be told.
With a wink and smile, they hold the line,
These quirky gems, so hard to find!

A Hidden Language of Pins

Pins like whispers, soft and sly,
They dance on jackets, oh my, oh my!
Each prick and poke, a clever jest,
A tiny drama, always dressed.

With lacquered shine, they giggle bright,
An ode to style, pure delight.
What do they say? Let's take a guess,
"Wear me well—don't be a mess!"

The Beauty of Forgotten Accessories

In boxes deep, they sleep away,
Forgotten friends, in disarray.
A dragonfly, a rusted clock,
Waiting for laughter, like a good ol' shock!

Rescue them all, let them shine,
Let quirky dreams intertwine.
A dance of dust, a comic spin,
With every pin, let joy begin!

A Touch of Whimsy

On the lapel, a curious bug,
Winks at me, gives a playful shrug.
A twinkle in its little eyes,
It laughs at fashion's silly ties.

A shimmering fish, it's all a joke,
Dancing there, a tiny bloke.
Wearing wonders, I strut and sway,
With critters that just want to play.

The Symbolism of a Small Silhouette

A tiny bird, with wings of flair,
Imitating a jump and a dare.
It chirps a tune, so fresh and bright,
A silly sight in morning light.

A wee cat grins, why so sly?
Pouncing on fabrics, oh my, oh my!
In every pin, a secret dance,
A giggle wrapped in a crafty chance.

Glimmers of Elegance

A sparkly gem, it's quite a tease,
It catches light, puts me at ease.
Winking softly, it holds its ground,
In the midst of laughter, it's joy unbound.

The diamond's glance can make you grin,
It knows how to reel you in.
With every twinkle, a playful jest,
In this fine game, I am a guest.

Adorning Shadows

In shadows deep, a critter lies,
Surprising all with its quirky guise.
A clever squirrel made of gold,
Tales of mischief silently told.

A pair of glasses, all askew,
They squint at life, a humorous view.
In every clasp, a story gleams,
A world of fun stitched in dreams.

Twinkling Sentinels

On my jacket, a sparkly plea,
A brooch winks back, oh so cheeky!
It's a tiny knight with a shiny sword,
Guarding my heart, never bored.

When I wear it, I feel so grand,
Like royalty, with jewels unplanned.
It balances on fabric, a jolly sight,
Make me giggle, day or night.

The Language of Pins

Whispers of pins, tucked away,
Gossiping secrets in a playful way.
One shows a cat, both sly and spry,
While another dreams of cake up high.

In meetings, they poke and prod my thoughts,
Remind me of laughter, not tied in knots.
Each twist and turn in a curious dance,
Making everyone steal a glance.

Fragments of History on Fabric

A button here, a clasp there,
Each one a story, a love affair.
Old grandma's pin with patriotic flair,
Sits on my coat, bold and rare.

From the past, they giggle and smirk,
Telling tales of treasured work.
With each new outfit, they unite,
In a patchwork of charm, pure delight.

Ornate Guardians of Grace

A butterfly lands on my lush lapel,
With shimmering wings, it seems to yell!
"I'm here for the fun, let's fly away,
Add some mischief to your day!"

They guard my outfit with flair and pride,
These ornate friends stand side by side.
With each little sparkle, they conspire,
To set my wardrobe on fire!

Glimmers of Adornment

A sparkling pin upon my coat,
It winks and twirls, a merry gloat.
A lady's laugh, a tiny cheer,
It whispers secrets, "I'm right here!"

With weathered gems in vibrant hues,
It jests and japes with silly cues.
A fashion faux pas? Not quite true,
It's a conversation starter too!

Secret Keeper on a Silk Dress

A brooch so bold on silken glide,
It holds my hopes, my secrets inside.
It tugs at threads, a playful tease,
"Don't spill the beans!" it seems to say.

A lady's flaw, or gem so grand?
With just a wink, it makes a stand.
It pins my laughter to the air,
A mischief-maker everywhere!

Enchantment Worn Close

Tucked close to heart, a sparkling feat,
A tiny goblin with quickened beats.
It giggles, dances, whispers loud,
Among the stars, it feels so proud!

A playful squirm on a dress so fine,
It claims its spot, oh how divine!
With each step, it twists and grins,
A royal jester, where joy begins.

A Memory Clipped in Place

Once lost in time, it found its way,
A memory clip that loves to play.
With every twinkle, tales unfold,
Of awkward dances, jokes retold.

It sparkles bright in daylight's beam,
A wink, a nudge, a shared dream.
This little piece, a humor streak,
A laugh, a smile, and then we peek!

Enchanted Pinpricks

On the lapel, a spark does dance,
A shiny thing, it takes a chance.
With every wink and every twirl,
It holds the gossip of the world.

A ladybug with sapphires bright,
Seduction in a pin; what a sight!
It whispers tales of love and lore,
While keeping secrets, evermore.

At tea, it winks at Mr. Fred,
Who drops his scone and turns to red.
A brooch can steal the mention, too,
While adding flair to all that you do.

So, in the joy of fabric pinned,
Life's little trinkets, never sinned.
With laughter stitched into the seams,
A pop of humor in our dreams.

A Glimmer of Connection

A sparkle here, a dazzle there,
What's that stuck upon her hair?
A playful clip or cheeky pin,
That sends the crowd into a spin.

A parrot perched with rhinestone eye,
Chirps out loud, oh me, oh my!
It's a gossip reel in metal form,
Worn with laughter, never worn.

While croissants crumble in a rush,
That brooch can cause a subtle hush.
With puns and quips and all in jest,
It brings the party to its best.

So, wear the bling and don't you fret,
For silver wings, we won't forget.
Life's a joke, a merry flight,
With gleaming pins that feel just right.

Fluttering Elegance

A shiny pin upon my chest,
It winks and sparkles, quite the jest.
A butterfly caught in a fancy dance,
It whispers secrets, gives a glance.

A quirky twist, that's how it goes,
With every wear, my outfit grows.
A laugh erupts when friends come near,
As I declare, 'This made my year!'

It's not just style, it's playfulness,
With every twist that brings me bliss.
On collar, scarf, or hat it stays,
A whimsical touch, in many ways!

So here's to pins that steal the show,
With quirks and giggles, watch them glow.
A flutter here, a shimmy there,
Tomorrow's wear? A wild affair!

The Soul of a Silhouette

In the corner, a shadow prowls,
A pin that laughs and softly growls.
It's shaping laughter in the air,
With an attitude that shouts, 'I dare!'

A curious kitty, a sly old fox,
Fastened firmly with rubber socks.
It blinks at me with jeweled eyes,
And plays for laughter, that's no surprise!

A comical twist at every look,
In my wardrobe, it'll find its nook.
Fashion's playground, it never fails,
With funny stories that it tells!

So let it sway, let it jiggle around,
My little friend, where fun is found.
An edgy shape, it draws a line,
Crafting stories, oh so fine!

A Flicker of Sentiment

A quick little catch upon my shirt,
It nudges my heart, it gives a flurt.
Wearing nostalgia upon my sleeve,
With every glance, a giggle I weave.

An old-school car, a cat with sass,
Pin it down, then watch it pass.
With every story, a chuckle blooms,
And funny tidings float through rooms.

It flickers bright with tales of yore,
This little piece makes me want more.
In moments shared, it likes to play,
Creating smiles, come what may!

So here's to laughter and a bit of flair,
With all the fun this brooch can share.
A treasure trove, with giggles abound,
In every turn, sweet joy is found!

Fastened Dreams

Oh, what a sight on my coat to see,
A pin that grins so joyfully!
It's like a clown in a tiny show,
Wobbling around to steal the glow.

Fasten it here or place it there,
Silly motifs, if you dare!
With a wink, it tells a tale,
Of adventures grand that cannot fail.

Giggles erupt when I strut and pose,
My outfit blooms with chuckles and prose.
Just when you think it's plain and tame,
It jumps to life with a funny name!

So let it ride, let the laughter flow,
With each new wear, the fun will grow.
In fastened dreams, where joy convenes,
A pin brings forth our silliest scenes!

Iconic Adornments

Once a lady wore a pin,
On her dress, it made a grin.
A giant fish, or so it seemed,
Surely not what she had dreamed.

Friends gathered 'round with laughs and cheer,
"Is that a fish?" they quipped in fear!
"At least it's stylish, that is true,"
She winked and said, "It's sushi too!"

Pins of Past and Present

A velvet jacket, a pin so bright,
Worn by grandma, a funny sight.
A dinosaur, all sparkly and green,
Oh, the fashion choices she did glean!

In photos, she strikes a pose so grand,
"This dino's fierce!" she waved her hand.
Yet years roll by, and what a scene,
That dino now is on her machine!

The Glow of a Timeless Piece

A gem encrusted on my coat,
It sparkles brightly, makes me gloat.
But watch it slip and give a roll,
Now it's a steampunk cannonball!

My friend just gasped, "What have you done?"
"A fashion statement! Isn't it fun?"
With each loud clink, I strut and sway,
"Who needs a job? I'm on display!"

Captivating Curiosities

What's that glimmer? Can't resist,
A quirky shape, you can't dismiss.
A squashed tomato, worn with pride,
Makes me the talk of the whole ride!

At lunch they ask, "Where's that from?"
"A thrift shop treasure, isn't it fun?"
I wink and munch, my accessory bold,
"Who needs gold when you've got the weird and old!"

Glinting Narratives

A shiny little story told,
It winks and jabs, a sight to behold.
On jackets, it plays hide and seek,
With laughter tucked on each little peak.

It twirls on collars, flips on ties,
Whispers tales through playful sighs.
A dragonfly or fragile flower,
Turns dull attire to vibrant power.

It dances on the chest with glee,
A tiny star in a fabric sea.
What charm lies in such small delight,
To turn a frown to pure delight.

Each pin a chuckle, a wry little pun,
A memory spark, oh, what fun!
In meetings or while shopping fast,
This sparkling rogue is unsurpassed!

The Allure of a Gathered Spark

A glimmer caught in the corner's eye,
A shiny secret, oh my, oh my!
Worn low or high, it steals the show,
With just a twist, off it can go.

An owl, a cat, or a quirky shoe,
It speaks a language both old and new.
With every clink, it spills a jest,
A trinket that never lets you rest.

An invite to laugh, a call to cheer,
An ornament close, keep it near!
It spins old tales in a modern way,
Turning serious into a playful sway.

On forget-me-nots and lapels so dear,
It brings a chuckle wrapped in cheer.
So find your spark, make it your own,
In laughter's light, never alone!

Memories Fastened

Fastened tight, a memory's muse,
Dancing on jackets, never to lose.
Each pin a story, each clasp a grin,
Unlocking laughs, let the fun begin!

In family photos, a playful tease,
Sipping laughter like herbal teas.
"Was that my hair?" comes the sly inquiry,
"Or just the brooch being a bit flirty?"

It jingles and jangles, oh what a sound,
In boredom's grip, it's truly profound.
A gem of wit, or a cheeky jest,
This quirky piece is quite the guest!

So throw it on with flair and style,
Let it shine brightly, make others smile.
Who knew such knickknacks could possess such cheer,
With every glance, they turn the year!

Jewel's Secret Ambiance

A secret keeper with a glint so sly,
It sits there proudly, oh me, oh my!
It knows the gossip before I do,
Filling the room with charm anew.

An acorn here or dragon's wing there,
Whispers of laughter linger in the air.
Tales of the past wrapped snug and tight,
Bringing joy with every twinkling light.

And just like that, a serious chat,
Turns to giggles with a simple spat.
The star of the show with no need to brag,
A tiny treasure in a fabric bag!

So treasure your pin, let it play,
Together we'll find a fun-filled way.
With every costume, each woman's pride,
This cheeky little bauble is best as your guide!

Adoring the Everyday

A little shimmer on my shirt,
It mildly screams, 'I'm not a flirt!'
With colors wild and shapes so neat,
It dances anytime I skip a beat.

Pin it high, or let it slide,
On a polka dot, it takes a ride.
My quirky friend, you get the show,
In all the places I won't go!

In morning light, it catches eyes,
Mocking muffins, sneers at pies.
Who knew such flair could come to play,
And make my breakfast feel so gay?

Oh jeweled wonder, hang around,
Let's see if you can turn this frown.
On my lapel, you're quite the tease,
With you, mundane is sure to please!

A Token of Grace

A little pin that sits so proud,
Among my clothes, it forms a crowd.
It's not a tree, it's not a star,
Yet in my heart, it travels far.

Once lost it seemed, among my socks,
Hiding there near old flip-flops.
But with a flourish, out it shone,
Proclaiming, 'Here, you're not alone!'

At family dinners, oh what fun,
It blinks and winks—'Come join the run!'
While Grandma's tales of youth unfold,
It giggles with the stories told.

So raise a glass, let's toast the day,
To this old token, hip and gay.
A whisper soft, a wink so nice,
With every outfit, it's more than spice!

The Quiet Allure of Jewelry

A shiny thing that tends to laugh,
Sits in the drawer, a real giraffe.
With snacks and sodas, it forms a crew,
Where else can such diversity brew?

Beneath the couch, it bounces bright,
A secret glee in morning light.
Perhaps it dreams of fancy balls,
But here at home, it trips and falls.

Worn to the park, it waves hello,
To all the pigeons strutting slow.
With every sway, it's full of cheer,
This silly little thing, oh dear!

As days go by, it starts to know,
Life's not just diamonds, but a show.
So here we dance, with life's embrace,
Embracing the odd, in perfect grace!

Ornate Echoes

A bauble bright that's lost its way,
Ends up on shirts like birds in play.
It marks the spot of where I stand,
A treasure map made by my hand.

On Mondays grumpy, it says, 'Smile!'
A radical gem most worth the while.
With every glance it starts a chat,
Saying, 'Look here, where's your hat?'

While others covet the gold and shine,
I just adore this quirky line.
A flip-flop here, a wink or two,
The laughter swirls like morning dew.

So when you spot this dazzling thing,
Remember joy, that's what it brings.
In every twist, a tale unfolds,
With all its quirks, it never folds!

Brooches of the Heart

On my jacket sits a cat,
With a wink and a silly hat.
It prances and wiggles about,
Leaving no room for a doubt.

Next to it, a dancing bee,
Buzzing as cute as can be.
It sticks like glue, won't depart,
Oh, the joy it brings to my heart!

A fish that jumps, oh so spry,
It flops and flitters, oh my, oh my!
With sequins that sparkle and gleam,
Who knew clothing could be a dream?

Chasing shadows, they play hide and seek,
Giggling away while I peek.
Every pin bears a tale or two,
Each day is brighter when I wear my crew.

A Pin with Purpose

A pin shaped like a slice of pie,
Always brings a smile, oh my!
Every bite's a tasty stunt,
Worn proudly on my shirt's front.

Next up, a quirky, tiny shoe,
It dances along, it's true.
With every step, it shakes and jives,
A dainty charm that truly strives.

Look at this bright little fish,
Giving my outfit a fanciful wish.
Swirling colors that make me grin,
It's the life of the party, where do I begin?

With a hat, a belt, a joy parade,
These little pals never fade.
They cheer me on when days are tough,
Wearing them makes life less rough.

Elegance in a Tiny Frame

In a tiny frame, a squirrel doth pose,
With acorns stacked and a nose that glows.
Dressed in jewels, it sways with flair,
Who knew such style could be so rare?

A little cupcake takes the stage,
With frosting bright, it's all the rage.
It's so sweet, it gives me glee,
Just a treat to wear, you see!

An owl with glasses reads a book,
In its wisdom, I take a look.
With each chapter, it gives a nod,
What a funny, tiny facade!

So when drabness starts to sneak,
I wear my friends, and they speak.
In colors and shapes, they shine so bright,
Creating laughter, pure delight.

Tales of Timeless Beauty

A prancing unicorn in a swirl,
Brings a giggle and a twirl.
With sparkles trailing on its tail,
It makes dull moments a fairytale.

A peacock struts, so bold and bright,
Wearing colors, what a sight!
Each feather tells a fancy tale,
In its presence, I cannot fail.

Tiny turtles, slow and sly,
On my lapel, they wave goodbye.
With little smiles, they say, 'Don't rush!'
In their chill vibe, I find the hush.

In a world of glitz and glee,
These trinkets are a jubilee.
With laughter and love, they bring to me,
A kaleidoscope of joy, so carefree!

Reflections in Embellishment

A shiny piece of trinket slips,
Hiding stories on its tips.
It blinks with laughter, catches eyes,
A quirky gem that never lies.

Pin it high or wear it low,
A conversation starter, you know?
With colors bright, it sways and twirls,
Among the crowd, it leaps and whirls.

From grandmas' gifts to thrift store finds,
Each one tells tales, oh so kind.
They giggle, wobble, dance about,
These little wonders we can't live without.

So as you strut your stuff with flair,
Remember that sparkle, that little dare.
An accessory to crown your lot,
In life's grand stage, it's all that you've sought.

Talismans of Affection

A secret keeper on my lapel,
With glittery tales it's sure to tell.
Hiding mischief, jest, and cheer,
This little buddy draws you near.

With winks and nods it plays a game,
Each tiny spark ignites the flame.
A lucky charm or just for show,
In every gathering, it steals the glow.

Friends gather 'round, they ask its name,
"Oh, who's the star?" they shout in fame.
With giggles loud, it holds its ground,
In silly lore, our laughs abound.

So wear it proud, let laughter flow,
A pin of fun, an inner glow.
In every fabric, let it seat,
For this wild ride is oh so sweet!

Accessories of Affinity

Each shiny piece, a little jest,
On my chest, it feels the best.
Like a best friend but made of gold,
A funny look, a tale retold.

It bounces on a button bright,
Daring everyone to laugh outright.
With colors loud and shapes so odd,
It's laughter's post, a giggle prod.

At parties wild, it takes the floor,
In joyful waves, it begs for more.
Oh, who needs jewels of grand design?
This quirky flair is simply divine.

So let's not take our pins too serious,
For every laugh makes life curious.
Embrace the odd, let it shine forth,
In the land of laughter, it's of great worth!

Pins of Poetic Expression

A pin that jests, a pin that gleams,
It thrives on laughter, grows on dreams.
With whimsy packed in every pose,
A silent shout that boldly shows.

It pops and sparkles with a grin,
A playful product, let's begin.
On lovely coats or just a hat,
This little pin is where it's at.

In gatherings where giggles fly,
It tells of joy without a sigh.
With every poke, we share a smile,
This tiny buddy walks in style.

So don your flair, let laughter blend,
For each small pin is a true friend.
In life's great tale of silly bliss,
These little treasures are hard to miss.

Embroidered Whispers

A tiny flower with a gleam,
It holds my secrets, or so it seems.
It winks at my shirt with playful grace,
And says, "Wear me now, off to the race!"

Each clasp and pin makes me feel bold,
Dressed to impress, or so I was told.
But sometimes it slips, like a sly little mouse,
And I laugh as it dances right out of my blouse!

Threads of Beauty

A sparkle here, a glint over there,
It sparkles like gossip, with flair to spare.
My vest was plain, but now it's a show,
It's like a Picasso, with color aglow!

Each stitch stirs giggles from those who see,
"What a fine mess!" they chuckle with glee.
But isn't that magic? To wear a delight?
To twinkle and shimmer, both day and night!

A Keepsake Celebrated

A treasure pinned, a day to remember,
This shiny gem can outshine December.
With every glance, a story it tells,
Of grandpas, grandmas, and mischief that swells!

It settles right snug on my collar's peak,
Then drags my shirt with a playful squeak.
"Oh dear!" I gasp as it starts to roam,
A rogue little keepsake, no longer at home!

The Language of a Lapel

There's chatter in the stitching, it's clear to me,
A button that bickers, oh what a spree!
With phrases like 'fabulous' that boldly parade,
While I stand by, just a bit bemused and dismayed.

A twist here, a turn there, oh what a show,
My outfit's now giddy, all dressed to glow!
It chuckles and jives with each little sway,
Who knew fashion could laugh in such a way?

The Allure of Little Things

A tiny sparkle on my chest,
It catches eyes, who'd think it best?
With colors bright, it starts to dance,
A bold statement, or just a chance?

In pockets deep, they hide away,
A brooch that's simply here to play.
It laughs at rules, it breaks the norm,
In each small clip, there's silly charm!

Unveiled Grace

Pin me on, I shout with glee,
A fluttering friend, oh can't you see?
With quirks and puns, I make a scene,
Enchanted moments, I'm the queen!

Adorn your coat, I do insist,
A pop of fun, one can't resist.
In gatherings, I steal the show,
With cheeky smiles, I steal the glow!

Brooches of Remembrance

They tell stories in little ways,
Of silly mishaps and wild days.
Each clip a memory, funny and bright,
In every corner, a laugh's in sight.

Pinned on with care, they come alive,
In retro styles, they still can thrive.
A wink, a nod, a playful tease,
These little gems are sure to please!

A Tale Embedded in Time

Once a present, now a tease,
In patches worn, it finds its breeze.
With stories tucked, it loves to spin,
A flick of laughter deep within.

From grandma's draw to modern flair,
This tiny art is simply rare.
With a twist, it brightens the room,
A playful dance, it does consume!

A Dance of Light and Metal

In a drawer beneath the socks,
A gathering of shiny rocks.
They twinkle bright, oh what a sight,
Worn by grannies with delight.

A dragonfly, a silly cat,
The queen of bling, a floppy hat.
Each pin tells tales, a laughing spree,
Fashion fun in irony.

They wiggle, jiggle with all their might,
On jackets bold, they take to flight.
Forget the trends, embrace the mess,
Brooches here, it's a fashion fest!

So raise a glass to all the odd,
Those quirky gems we love and prod.
In this metal dance, we'll twirl and sway,
Let laughter shine on brooches' play!

Sentimental Stitches

Tucked within a patchwork quilt,
A spider brooch with threads so built.
It laughs at time, it stitches back,
In memory lane, it finds the knack.

A pin shaped like an old-time phone,
Reminds us all of days alone.
The dial spins tales of yesteryears,
And still brings smiles instead of tears.

With every whim, we change our gear,
A butterfly pinned brings us near.
To remind us of the glee we had,
These little quirks make life not sad.

So treasure each little motif,
In metallic joy, let's find relief.
For each small piece holds laughter tight,
With every wear, it feels just right!

Adorning Stories Untold

Oh, what tales these trinkets weave,
In gatherings where we believe.
A starfish brooch, a red-hot chili,
   Each one giggles, oh so silly.

From hunters' vests to wedding gowns,
These quirky charms turn frowns to crowns.
What's next, I wonder, from a thrift store bin?
   A pizza slice, let's pin that in!

They sit and wait, those sparkling gems,
With hopes to shine on ladies' hems.
In bathroom chats, they join the fun,
   Our laughter's echo — a brooch's run.

So when in doubt, just pin it right,
Adorn yourself; what a great sight!
Whimsical adventures await, my friend,
   With every brooch, the smiles extend!

Tiny Treasures in the Shadows

Deep in the corner, what do I spy?
A quirky pin, oh my, oh my!
With a googly eye and pom-pom tail,
It surely tells a giggly tale.

A tiny thimble with a grin,
Worn to remind us where we've been.
In closet depths, the jests unfold,
Unruly ornaments of stories bold.

The penguin wears a monocle,
While frogs in crowns feel quite magical.
Each treasure bursting with a jest,
Who knew that odd could be the best?

So here's to trinkets, small and bright,
In shadows cast by day and night.
Let laughter reign and fashion thrive,
With tiny treasures, we come alive!

Twinkles on Tartan

A dainty sparkle, pin it right,
Catching eyes in morning light.
Hiding secrets in its gleam,
Winking softly, like a dream.

Flaps of fabric, bold and grand,
Tartan struts, with flair you'll stand.
But oh dear, what's that you say?
Is it stuck? Please save the day!

It twirls and dances on your chest,
In plaid and plaid, it's quite the jest.
With every wiggle, laugh it brings,
Just don't let it catch your wings!

A pin on cap and shoes so neat,
Granny's gift, a timeless treat.
With every glance, a giggle sprouts,
Fashion's whimsy, without doubts.

The Brocade of Memories

A shimmer bright, a tale untold,
Wrapped in fabric, memories old.
Each brocade stitch tells a jest,
Of shifting styles and fashion quests.

A grandma's clasp, a smile so wide,
Caught in time, the joy won't hide.
When you wear it, laughter flows,
Making mischief wherever it goes.

Pinned on jackets, hats, and more,
It sparkles still, like days of yore.
In velvet touch, the playful sighs,
As styles change, so do the ties.

Much like socks that don't quite match,
It holds sweet tales, a hidden batch.
A treasure chest upon your chest,
A giggle waiting, jest expressed.

Stars Stitched in Silence

Underneath the evening glow,
A pin awaits, just thought I'd show.
Stars stitched close, they laugh and wink,
In silence dance, they hardly blink.

A quirky shape, it bears no fear,
It proudly shouts, 'Come look right here!'
On collars fine, it's quite a sight,
Who knew stars could be so light?

Each twinkle giggles, bends a bit,
Hilarity when it decides to sit.
With every wrinkle, tales unfold,
Jokes from days both fresh and old.

Onward it marches, if it could,
Showing off how well it stood.
With every shuffle and every boast,
In life's great party, it's the host!

A Heartbeat on the Chest

With every step, it beats and sways,
A bouncing heart that seeks to play.
Clipped on tight, a fun parade,
In fashion's court, it's grandly laid.

It mimics life, a heartbeat's race,
A joyful wink upon your face.
Some may find it odd and bizarre,
But who'd not want a flashy star?

When you forget your very style,
Just clip it on, wear it with a smile.
A giggle's worth, a playful jest,
You'll turn each day into a fest.

Bound in laughter, bright in jest,
Worn proudly—it outshines the rest.
So hold it close, let others see,
A heartbeat's charm, pure jubilee!

A Touch of Vintage Splendor

In a drawer, tangled dreams lie,
A battered pin, it winks sly.
A lady once wore it with pride,
Now it's just a quirky guide.

Bright colors shout, 'I'm here to play!'
Faded whispers, once in the fray.
With pearls that mimic a fat cat's purr,
It gallops through time, there's quite a stir.

Oh, the stories it must hold tight,
Of mismatched socks and dance floor fright.
A noisy laugh at a boring lunch,
Or a wink from a past, soft as a punch.

So raise your glass to this bold delight,
An oddity that just feels right.
With each little spark, it steals the show,
Who knew a pin could steal the glow?

Timeless Spark on the Lapel

A twinkle sits upon my coat,
Like a pirate's parrot afloat.
It clings on tight, my sidekick true,
With a wink, it shouts, 'Look at you!'

The crowd may glance, a fleeting stare,
At shimmering gold that flashes flair.
Just a reminder, life's a jest,
Wear your joy, it's simply the best!

Sometimes it tumbles, sometimes it spins,
Catching all with sparkling grins.
It teeters there, oh what a sight,
Making dull days just feel bright.

So don your lapel with a cheeky flair,
Join the fun, if you dare.
With a little pin, you can ignite,
Every moment, make it light!

The Elegance of Resilience

Once dropped twice, it still won't flee,
Like a stubborn gnome, it sticks with glee.
A dash of flair, a sprinkle of sass,
It twirls and jigs; it's never crass.

Worn by grandmas and crafty chums,
It laughs at age, how it hums!
With sparkles glowing, a diva's dance,
Who knew this pin could take a stance?

Oh, how it jives at mundane affairs,
With originality that dares and dares.
Each twist and turn, it plays so well,
A classic tale, but who can tell?

So here's to pins, both odd and grand,
Each a unique story, each a brand.
In every fluster, mischief unruly,
This little buddy makes life truly silly!

Memories Cloaked in Color

A pop of red, a wink of blue,
It struts in style; oh, who knew?
With buttons and bows, it teases fate,
A memory wraps around, never late.

In family photos, it steals the show,
Dressed on jackets from long ago.
With each glance, chuckles emerge,
At fashion disasters that still surge.

So let it shine at the town parade,
With sparkles dancing, brigades to invade.
A gleeful cheer from times quite past,
In the garden of memory, it's sure to last.

So if you've got one, wear it proud,
Join the laugh, join the crowd.
For every piece has a story to tell,
In colors bright, we'll laugh and dwell!

The Art of Embellishment

A shiny piece that catches light,
It winks at me from morning till night.
"Look at me!" it seems to say,
"I make your outfit less gray!"

Dressed up in colors, oh so bright,
Does it make sense? Not quite right!
Yet here it sits, a curious friend,
A fashion choice that won't quite end.

A quirky pin upon my chest,
It holds my secrets, it loves the jest.
A story told with every glance,
In this wild fashion dance!

Who knew a trinket could cause such glee?
With one small push, it sets me free.
It giggles and spins, a playful tease,
Leaving behind style critiques — a breeze!

Beneath the Surface of Style

Below the sparkle, there's so much more,
Like an ocean hiding treasures galore.
A pin that once was just a dull thing,
Now twirls and leaps like it's got wings!

A cat in a hat? A fish in a shoe?
Each piece reveals a laugh or two.
It might seem silly, yet here we are,
Wearing our madness, oh how bizarre!

Accessorizing a tee with flair,
People stare and stop for air.
Is that a UFO? No, just my brooch!
The universe laughs — oh coach, oh coach!

So pin it on, don't be shy!
Let your wild side touch the sky.
Life is short, much like my rhyme,
So let's bedazzle, one more time!

Captured Moments in Enamel

In enamel hues, the past is caught,
Memories saved, never forgot.
A dog in a bowtie, a cat in a bow,
Every glance at it puts on a show.

With every shimmer, a giggle bursts,
Who knew such things would quench my thirst?
For fun and laughter, sparkle and shine,
My wacky embellishment is just divine!

Let's gather 'round for a cheeky toast,
To the quirkiest treasures we love the most.
A pin that tells tales of joy and woe,
Each twinkle urging us to go, go, go!

In a world that can sometimes frown,
This gadget gives all a reason to clown.
So here's to the stories that brooches share,
A laugh, a style, a memory rare!

The Stories We Wear

On a collar or a lapel, we place our tales,
Jokes and giggles held by tiny nails.
A horse, a hat, a fish, or a star,
Each tells a story, oh so bizarre!

They hang like laughter, they dance with flair,
Bringing delight to the plainest wear.
With a wink and a nudge, they say, "Come see!"
Let's celebrate this absurdity!

With friends all around, we snicker and cheer,
At the wonders of fashion that tickle our year.
Who needs gold when you've got a clown?
Embellished moments blend up and down!

So let's choose glamour with a pinch of fun,
Wearing our whimsy — oh, we have won!
In every sparkle, a hearty laugh,
Life's more delightful with a brooch on the path!

Caught in the Thread of Time

A little pin that's lost its way,
Stuck on a sweater, here to stay.
It smiles crookedly at the logs,
A fashion statement for the frogs.

Under the bed, it had a ball,
Belting out tales with a dustbunny thrall.
Through thick and thin, it took the ride,
A sparkly ghost we can't abide.

It haunted us at the yard sale,
Still held fast by a pointy tail.
"Oh, don't you look quaint!" we all agreed,
As it winked at the vintage bead.

At parties, it's quite the show,
With sneezes and laughs, it steals the glow.
Though trendy's a term that's ceased to be,
This little guy still rides with glee.

A Dance of Gems and Metals

Oh, what a waltz in the jewelry box,
Where a diamond's winking at the old fox.
With a shimmy and shake, they swirl and twirl,
Creating chaos in a shiny whirl.

The gold one trips and catches its breath,
While silver giggles, flirting with death.
"Watch me!" cries ruby, "I'm the best!"
"Not so fast, dear! You're just a guest!"

Emerald laughs and climbs up high,
As garnet sighs, "I'm telling a lie."
A dance so bright, it fills the night,
Who knew jewels had such appetite?

In jumbled colors and wild designs,
They sparkle like spark plugs, they shine like signs.
On a lapel or dress so grand,
They throw a party across the land.

Forgotten Adornments

In a drawer where secrets lay,
A button and clasp have come to play.
"They said I was trendy, oh what a hoot!
Now I'm just dust with a stubborn root."

A resin cat thinks it's a queen,
With faux pearls that glow in shades of green.
"It's a vintage look!" the cat purred loud,
Caught in a selfie, feeling so proud.

A tiny frog with a gem-studded crown,
Hopes for a fairytale, won't let down.
But in the drawer, it cannot leap,
Just dreams of a pond where memories sleep.

They giggle and chuckle, these remnants of flair,
When fashion comes back, will they get a share?
Or are they to linger, forgotten, pristine?
Stuck in that drawer, oh, what could have been!

A Timeless Embrace

A clasp like a hug from a friend so dear,
Holding memories with a pointed cheer.
"A little snug," it claims with pride,
Embracing the fabric like a joyful ride.

Each pin tells a story from days gone past,
With glittering laughter that's meant to last.
"Look at me shine!" cried the brooch on the coat,
"So stylish and grand, I'm the best thing afloat!"

At the family gathering, it steals the scene,
With snickers and jokes, it feels so keen.
Unruly and wild, a brooch with a joke,
Wrapping memories tighter than a family cloak.

In ridiculous shapes, they charm and delight,
From a seahorse to a dragon, oh what a sight!
Forever embraced, they sparkle true,
In the game of fashion, they'll woo and pursue.

The Revival of Antiquity

In a dusty old box, what do I see?
A relic from ages, quite fancy and free.
It sparkles and winks, with a grin on its face,
I try it on now; oh what style, what grace!

Grandma's old treasures are all coming back,
With colors so bright, they could shock an old tack.
I wear it to dinner and chaos unfolds,
As it catches the light—everyone scolds!

My friend claims it's cursed, a hex from the past,
But I just can't resist; I'm having a blast!
It jabs at my chest like a pesky old bee,
Is this fashion or madness? Who needs to agree?

So here's to the past, let's wear it with pride,
A pin from the attic, a colorful ride.
We giggle and laugh, what a wild little trend,
Antiquity's back, just don't take it to bend!

The Allure of Delicate Designs

A tiny pink flower with a sparkly heart,
Clings tightly to fabric like a kid with a tart.
It whispers, 'Wear me!' in a voice so polite,
But I'm paranoid—what if it takes flight?

The cat's very curious, swats at the clasp,
I shoo it away with a flick of my gasp.
Do these trinkets have powers? Oh dear, what if so?
I'd rather stick to cupcakes with frosting to show!

At lunch with my buddies, it steals all the shine,
They laugh and they joke, 'You're a fashion divine!'
But wait, what's that smell? A scent from my sneeze?
Oh no, the flower's attracted the bees!

So delicate treasures, I solemnly vow,
I'll wear you with pride—until I endow.
But please, let's agree, no more games or wild dreams,
Just you, me, and cupcakes, forget all extremes!

A Loving Pinch

My brooch is a pinch, with a pinch more of fun,
Daring the world to compare, just for the pun.
It's a chicken with bling, what a comical sight,
My friends can't stop giggling, it's too much delight!

It's perched on my sweater, strutting its stuff,
Onlookers perplexed, this is more than enough!
$20 at a yard sale, what a steal, what a find,
Now it rules all my outfits, oh eyes, never blind!

With humorous glances and laughter aloud,
My quirky old chicken, it makes me so proud.
A statement of fun, not just any dull flair,
It dances through life on the edge of my wear.

So, pinch me again if it's all just a dream,
This chicken's my partner, we're quite the team.
Together we're silly, forever we'll twine,
A loving little pinch, oh how it does shine!

Twinkling Tales

Once upon a time, in a jewelry box,
Lived a star-shaped brooch with a glittery frocks.
It dreamed of adventures, oh how it would gleam,
'This plot twist is daring; wait, or is it a theme?'

Opacity loves it, but clarity's mad,
They fight 'til the morning and keep going bad.
'The choice is so tough!' whispers big carat ring,
And everyone giggles at the chaos they fling.

One day they all wandered to a fancy old fair,
The brooch made a speech—'Life beyond this wear!'
As it twinkled and twirled, smiles spread like the sun,
These trinkets of laughter found life had begun.

Now they all unite in the name of pure fun,
With tales of wild nights when they've just come undone.

Crafted stories that glitter with humor and glee,
In a sparkle-filled world, just you wait and see!

Potions of Beauty

A little pin, so bright and gay,
Grows fancier with each passing day.
It dons a hat, it wears a shoe,
Sometimes a cat, sometimes a shoe!

With sparkly gems that giggle and dance,
Each twist and turn, a silly prance.
Oh, how it winks, this brooch of mine,
A tiny jester, oh, so divine!

It tells me tales of nights a-glow,
Of parties grand and frolic below.
Your grandma wore it, they say with glee,
But I wear it now, just wait and see!

In pockets deep or on a sleeve,
It's quite the thing that I believe.
It gives me charm, it gives me grace,
A quirky smile on my face!

A Glint of History

A dainty piece from days of yore,
Sparkles bright, oh, what a score!
It traveled far on someone's dress,
Now sits with me, oh, what a mess!

A million stories in each tiny crack,
Of ballrooms filled and a dance attack.
Once a crown for a queen's attire,
Now a paperweight or some new fire!

It whispers secrets of gossip shared,
And how many hearts it might have snared.
Did it hold a letter, or maybe a tear?
Oh, the juiciest bits, come gather near!

In this glimmer lies so much cheer,
A relic that moves me, that's quite clear.
Imagine the gowns, the laughter and fun,
And now it's mine, oh, what a run!

Artistry in a Small Frame

A tiny canvas, such a small face,
Crafted with care, it takes its place.
It hangs about, with flair so bold,
Whispers of art that's never old.

Each curve and twist, a playful jest,
It dreams of being a fancy vest.
But instead, it's nestled just so,
On jackets, bags, wherever I go!

It giggles when worn, a mischievous tease,
A slice of charm that aims to please.
I chuckle loud as it catches the light,
A little artist, what a delight!

In crowds it stands, a solo show,
Painting my day with a friendly glow.
The critics scoff, but who's to blame?
This tiny frame, oh, it's got fame!

Echoes of Elegance

Tucked in the folds of a dress so fine,
A splash of whimsy, a dab of shine.
It struts around with fanciful glee,
Daring all hats to challenge its spree!

With every step, a giggle it sends,
A chorus of joy that never ends.
It hums a tune of days gone by,
In ludicrous ways, oh, my oh my!

From opulent halls to casual scenes,
It elevates life, if you know what I mean!
A wink here, a nudge there, it knows its role,
Making me laugh, oh, what a goal!

So here's to the echo of what it brings,
A wink of laughter, oh, how it sings!
In this tiny dance of endless tease,
Echoes of elegance, bring me to my knees!

Graceful Emblems

Upon my lapel, a strange bug sits,
Looks like it lost its way in fits.
With a wink and a twist, it proudly beams,
A fashion choice beyond my wild dreams.

It sparkles like stars in a night so clear,
Whispers of style, oh dear, oh dear!
My friend's eyes bulge, she can't stop to stare,
Is it art, or a critter too bold to wear?

With each tiny glance, laughter erupts,
My pin's a comedian, no room for hiccups.
Yet here we stand, a duo in bliss,
Who knew a brooch could cause such a fuss?

Dancing with flair from my coat, it sways,
Making up stories in whimsical ways.
Is it a treasure or just a gaffe?
In the end, we all end up in a laugh!

Symbols of Strength and Grace

A gem adorned on my chest, oh what a tease,
It boldly declares, 'I've tamed the breeze!'
But really, dear friend, it's just a bright pin,
Round and shiny, my fashionable grin.

With a quirky smile, it whispers to me,
'Why not wear a bird or a fancy old bee?'
So I strut down the street with a grin on my face,
No one knows I'm just clutching my space.

People pass by with their serious looks,
Not knowing this brooch is writing our books.
When it sings out, 'Life's just a game,'
I nod my head, embracing the fame.

With laughter we shine through the randomness,
This accessory speaks of pure happiness.
So here's to the sparkles that float in the air,
In a world full of boring, let's wear a fair share!

The Legacy of the Adorned

An heirloom passed down from my great aunt Lou,
A masterpiece made of mismatched blue.
It might be a treasure, or that's just my scheme,
A quirk in genealogy, or so it would seem.

Mom said it's precious, a family delight,
But on my blouse, it looks quite a fright.
With every unveiling, it tells us a tale,
That sometimes a brooch should just end up in jail!

As friends gather 'round with giggles galore,
We debate 'Is it art, or a decorative chore?'
With its awkward angles and odd, shiny flair,
It's more than a piece—it's a laugh to declare.

Yet amid the jest, there's a shimmer divine,
Linking past to present, through laughter we shine.
So here's to the pins that twinkle and tease,
Both lineage and laughter put us at ease!

A Brocade of Sentiment

A quirky attachment, oh my, such a sight,
With a twirl and a flick, it dances in light.
It shouts, 'I'm special, just look at my bling!'
But frankly, it's just like a butterfly's fling.

Upon my sweater, it joins the parade,
Like a confident wizard, it's daring and made.
To escape from the norm, it proudly stands tall,
In a world gone serious, it's the life of the ball!

Oh, the stories it brings with each clink and jingle,
A wacky collector's item that makes my heart tingle.
Among pearls and diamonds, it's the joker of decks,
Even on days when I wear mismatched socks!

So let's celebrate pins adorned with a laugh,
In a world where we worry, let joy lead the path.
For in every glittering piece that we wear,
Lives a giggle, a wink, and a story to share!

Whimsy in the Fabric of Life

In a drawer so chock-full, oh what a sight,
Lurks a pin with a cat, quite out of the light.
It twirls on my jacket, a most curious thing,
Does it think it's a bird? Oh, how it can sing!

Dancing on fabric, it has quite a flair,
Whispering secrets of times filled with care.
Each shiny little gem, with a wink and a grin,
Tells tales of wild parties where mischief did win.

A clown with a nose, so ludicrous bright,
Caught in a tussle with leftover pie bite.
Some look down their noses, call it a disgrace,
But I laugh at their frowns, while I sport it with grace!

So here's to the pins that we wear with delight,
Sprawled on our coats as they twinkle at night.
They're funny, they're quirky, and oh so absurd,
In this vast fabric, they're joyously heard!

Adornments of the Heart

A daisy, a dragonfly, all in a row,
Spellbinding the onlookers, don't you know?
Each trinket a memory, absurd yet so bright,
Worn with laughter, while causing a fright!

A brooch shaped like coffee, oh, what a thrill,
Sip me in style, it says with a quirked quill.
Friends chuckle and giggle, they can't help but tease,
"Are you feeling tired? Or just full of ease?"

A heart with a mustache, so comically bold,
Defying the norm, it could never be sold.
Yet in the right light, it just brings on cheer,
Who knew little bits could make such dear gear?

From kitties to cupcakes, they're all on display,
A laugh for each moment, come what may.
So let's strut our style, with humor and grace,
For life's a mad show; wear a smile on your face!

A Cluster of Memories

A broccoli brooch? Why yes, indeed,
With sparkles so bright, it plants quite a seed.
What a way to remind me to eat my greens,
While poking fun at all my silly routines!

A fuzzy pink bunny is all set to play,
Booming with laughter throughout the long day.
Friends spot it and chuckle, "What a delight!"
Who knew a pin could spark such a light?

Memories jingle like keys on a ring,
Every little piece makes my heart   sing.
A vintage old snoopy, it winks with a tease,
Says, "Wear me with joy, oh, do it with ease!"

Each pin tells a story, a chuckle here, there,
Adorning my outfits with whimsy and flair.
Let's gather and giggle, raise glasses up high,
To clusters of laughter that float through the sky!

Touchstones of Affection

A badge with a turtle? Quite the slow chap,
Looks like he's late for some fashionable nap.
But oh, when he smiles, he's a beacon of cheer,
Bringing all the giggles from far and near!

He stands on my collar, strutting in style,
While people do double-takes, stopping a while.
They muse, "What's the story behind such a piece?"
It whispers sweet secrets, a friendship's release!

Then there's a pin shaped like a curious fish,
Swimming through memories, granting each wish.
Oh, the tales it could tell of splashes and jumps,
While I keep on wearing it, trying to stumps!

With each little gem, my heart feels so light,
Adventures and laughter, vivid and bright.
So here's to the trinkets that dance in our life,
Poking fun with a wink, amid struggle or strife!

An Eloquent Fastening

A shiny pin with tales to share,
It holds the fabric of my flair.
With laughter, it clings, a trusty mate,
A fabric hug that's just first-rate.

It's not just metal, oh no, my friend,
It holds my style, it makes amends.
When shirts go wild, it steps in bold,
An anchor for the stories told.

It dances here, it skips right there,
A tiny jester without a care.
With every poke, it says "hey you,"
And reminds me of the joy I brew!

So here's to you, oh shiny thing,
A tiny icon, a playful ring.
With every fastened, clumsy jest,
You steal the show, I must confess!

Intricate Shapes of Splendor

Oh look at that, a twisty swan,
Who knew such art could be so fun?
With feathered curls and sparkly shine,
It's like it's trying to out-dine wine!

A bumblebee with jeweled wings,
It buzzes joy, and oh, it sings.
With every glance, a giggle, too,
It flits about in a funny hue.

An overgrown flower with a grin,
It's laughing hard, oh where to begin?
With petals wide and colors bright,
It makes the world feel more upright!

To wear a piece that's full of laugh,
Is like a kid in a sweet craft.
So let it be, this joyful spark,
On my lapel, it leaves its mark!

A Little Light Within

A glimmer caught in a mix of threads,
A tiny fire where laughter spreads.
With every twinkle, it wins the day,
A gentle nudge, come out to play!

A winking star upon my chest,
It whispers tales, not one repressed.
With every turn, it beams and shouts,
"Here I am!", no doubts about!

It's just a spark, yet so profound,
A beacon where my fun is found.
When moods are gray, it brings a smile,
And makes the world feel worthwhile!

So here's to light in silly places,
It dances through in funny spaces.
With every giggle, every fit,
This little light, it sure is lit!

Secrets Stitched in Time

A little patch of history here,
It folds my woes and quells my fear.
With every stitch, a secret's spare,
It tells of laughter, joy, and care.

A time-traveler on my sleeve,
It holds my past, it makes believe.
With layers deep and colors bright,
How did it get that froggy bite?

It whispers tales of days gone by,
Of awkward moments, oh my, my!
With every glance, a giggle bursts,
A patchwork world where joy immerses!

So here's to you, my vintage friend,
With horns and hats, you never bend.
A repository of laughter's bloom,
Stitched up together in this room!

www.ingramcontent.com/pod-product-compliance
Lightning Source LLC
Chambersburg PA
CBHW070315120526
44590CB00017B/2683